Sophie's Song

A True Christmas Story of Love, Faith, Prayer, Community, and Healing

Written By:
CHAD FELLOWS

Balboa Press books may be ordered through booksellers or by contacting:

Balboa Press
A Division of Hay House
1663 Liberty Drive
Bloomington, IN 47403
www.balboapress.com
844-682-1282

Sophie's photo on title page credit: Ann-Marie Vannucci of AMVphotography Inc.

Edited by Paula Diaco

ISBN: 978-1-9822-6109-2 (sc)
ISBN: 978-1-9822-6110-8 (e)
ISBN: 978-1-9822-6441-3 (hc)

Library of Congress Control Number: 2021903355

Print information available on the last page.

Balboa Press rev. date: 03/05/2021

BALBOA.PRESS
A DIVISION OF HAY HOUSE

Acknowledgements

How can I possibly acknowledge everyone involved in Sophie's story? We began to write names down for gifts sent to her in the hospital, but between watching over her, figuring out life details, and all the other letters, cards, and internet messages...we lost track. I want to thank each person who took a moment to wish her well and lighten our load.

First, to my wife Aimee, you are Sophie's earthly Angel in charge. You are a magnificent mother and my Too-Good-To-Be-True forever companion. Thank you for your watchful eye and invaluable intuition.

Each one of my children play an intricate role to Sophie and my life. To Judd, Claire, and Lucy...I love you much more than I can express.

To the following and to those I missed, you had a lasting impact on us. Sophie will realize your charity more as she gets older. I am thankful for people like you. I believe you each received blessings from God for reaching out to another in need and taking the time to make a difference. That never goes unnoticed or unrewarded. May you have the strength and understanding in your own challenges. We love you!

Abe Lindman
Abigail Evans
Adam and Dori Bowman Family
Aiden Brace
Alan Mullen
Alix Generous
All who followed her story on
    CaringBridge.org

All who posted in Thumbs Up 4 Sophie
    Facebook page!
Amanda Voyer
Ashley and Nancy Shamp
Axel and Amy Arnold family
Baileys
Becky and Jason Eberhard
Belisle Family

Benson Family
Bever Family
Bishop and Tiffany Rinne
Blake and Debbie Costley Family
Boston Children's Hospital staff
Brad and Linda Fellows Family
Bradley Friesen, MD
Brenda Simon
Bret & Angela Weekes
Brian and Nicole Groves
Bryan and Christy Clark
Cara Caswell & Sawyer Judkins
Carol Hurn
Carolyn Bever's Violin Group
Carrie and John Anderson
Chadwick Family
Chittenden Family
Chris & Meg Rosenbaum
Chris, Hannah, and Knightley Kirkpatrick
Clark & Bev Doney
Cohen Family
Connor Family
Corey and Nona Combe Family
Costco employees, Colchester, VT
Cris LaPierre
Cui Family
Cummings Family
Dave and Erin Larsen

Denise Jaques
Eberhard Family
Emily Shaw
Essex Ward, Montpelier Stake, LDS
    church
Evan Allen (Boston Globe)
First Congregational church, Essex VT
Gartland Family
Hamblin Family
Heidi Turner
Heidi Whitten
Hutchinson Family
Inland Hills Church
Irene Sege
Izzo Family
Jack Harper
Jack Welsh
Jackie Lincoln
Jacob and Heather Dahle
Jan Wilkinson
Jane Molofsky
Jane and Kai Fife-Pearson
Janet Nemeth
Jeanette Frotten
Jeannine Bourassa
Jeff McKinney
Jen and Joe Devita-O'Brien family
Jen, Nick, and Emma Charboneau

Jennifer Gariety & staff at EyeFellows
Jill Romanelli
Jim and Mary Whitten
Jo Barretto
Joanne Jewell
John and Diane Combe Family
John and Jamie Ellis
John Grimes
Julianna Battig
Julie Gussenhoven
Karen & Brad Garff
Kathie Hall
Kathy Oliver
Keith Karpinski & Family
Keith McGilvery
Ken and Kristie Bush (saved Lucy and I, stranded in a winter storm Northfield, VT while commuting from BCH)
Kim & Joe Staples
LDS missionaries of Tempe, AZ mission
Leavey Family
Leona and Gene Terry
Les and Lucille Ingram Family
Lesley Kwan, OD
Liliana Goumnerova, MD
Linda Hayes
Linda Wagner

Lindy Conroe
Loriann Taylor
Lynn & Geniel Fife Family
Mallett's Bay Elementary staff, teachers, and students especially Kate Ellingson and her fellow 4th graders! Heather Longchamp, Mrs Miller, principle Julie Benay, nurse Josie, and many more)
Marianne Cahill
Marie Agan (started Thumbs Up 4 Sophie Facebook page!)
Marci O'Neill, OD
Martha Thompson
McIntyre Family
Megan Leibovitz
Melanie and Shawn Hales
Melissa, Dave, and Mackenzie Mazza-Paquette
Merry Ann and Dave Gilbert
Michelle Reynolds
Mike Anderson
Milloy Family
Miriam March
Ms Carney
Ms Peggy Saicoe
Napolitano Family
Nate and Amy Madsen

Norma and Jon Ojala

North Country Federal Credit Union, Colchester

North Eagle Child Care...Mary Ellen

Old Colony Yacht Club, Dorchester, MA

Ophthalmic Consultants of Vermont

Paige Adams

Pam Anderson

Parascando Family

Patti McClure

Pearson Family

Peggy Aldous

Perry family (Kristy, Todd, Nick, Erin)

Phyllis Palmer

Pines Senior Living Community

Pizzagalli Family

Poorehouse family

Profaizer Family

President Bret Weekes and family

R.S and K.S. Williams

Rabidoux Family

Rhett Price Band

Rod & Tonya Stout

Ronald McDonald House, Brookline, MA

Russo family (Nicole, Tim, Owen)

Sara Bokelberg

Sara and Eli Morey

Scott and Annette Davis

Sean and Apryl Larkin

Sean and Molly Macardle

Snyder Family

Sorrell family

Spencer and Tonessa Andreason

St Albans Branch, Montpelier Stake, LDS Church

Stranger (firefighter) that came to hospital to give Sophie a Vermont Teddy Bear

Sue Warmoth

Tim and Amelia Holden

Tina Tuttle and Family

UVM Children's Hospital Team

Valerie Fitzgerald

Vermont Air Nat'l Guard MDG

WCAX News Cast

Weston Fisher

Will and Angie Fagan

Yawkeye House, Brookline MA

Zella and Day Bassett

Special Thanks

As a recipient of charitable generosity, our hearts will forever be full from the help we received from the following:

RONALD MCDONALD HOUSE. We abruptly moved our lives from Colchester, VT to Boston Massachusetts. We were able to stay in the Ronald McDonald house for several weeks. Food and other donations are continuously brought to the house to help those families staying there because of sick children. It was a place of comfort and within walking distance to Boston Children's Hospital. When asked what the community could do back in Colchester, VT for our family, I replied with a link of items the Ronald McDonald house needed from their website. The Colchester community paid for and donated everything on Ronald McDonald's list. Years later, I still remain in awe at the many interwoven stories of community service and love that was poured out to our family, or in behalf of Sophie.

Please consider donating to any Ronald McDonald House.

https://www.rmhc.org/

NOTE: The Ronald McDonald House where we stayed is now The Boston House, carrying on the legacy of caring for the families of children with bone marrow or stem cell treatments (https://www.thebostonhouse.org/).

BOSTON CHILDREN'S HOSPITAL (BCH). When they told us nine of the best neuro surgeons in the world were meeting to determine who would be the best doctor for Sophie, we were humbled and grateful to be at this amazing facility that helps treat and care for children worldwide. This place became our temporary second home. FIVE STAR HOSPITAL

Please consider donating to BCH or your local children's hospital. More hospitals need intraoperative MRI units that allow a surgeon to do an MRI during brain surgery. These units are $10 million or more each and not only save lives, but save children like Sophie from severe, life-altering brain damage due to surgery difficulties.

https://www.childrenshospital.org/ways-to-help

MAKE A WISH. After we were home from rehab, Sophie was weak but recovering. A friend introduced us to Make-A-Wish foundation. They granted Sophie a wish to go on a family Disney cruise. Our son was on a two year religious mission during Sophie's tumor and we were able to reunite and have a healing family vacation together on a once-in-a-lifetime Disney Cruise. Being close with family after this trauma was invaluable for us. We now support Make-A-Wish.

Please consider donating to Make-A-Wish foundation to help other families in times of heartache.

https://wish.org/

CAROLYN BEVER STUDIOS. Carolyn Bever is our dear friend and Sophie's amazing violin teacher. She rallied her violin families and students to drive in a snow storm to Boston Children's Hospital to finish Sophie's concert that she abruptly left the week before due to a severe headache. The impact of seeing those violinists and families in support of Sophie was priceless. The hospital concert was the night before Sophie's first brain surgery and we did not know if Sophie would ever be the same. Thank you a million times over Carolyn Bever.

MALLETT'S BAY ELEMENTARY. Sophie and her sister, Lucy were in 4th and 5th grade at Mallett's Bay. Kate Ellingson and Stephanie Miller visited Sophie in BCH. They were supportive to Sophie (and Lucy). But not just them, the principal Julie Benay and the entire school staff showed us so much love. Students made cards, people prayed for us, they did service at our home, and reached out on social media. We will never be able to say enough good things about the people at this Colchester, VT school.

RELIGIOUS ORGANIZATIONS. We are members of the Church of Jesus Christ of Latter Day Saints. We felt huge support from our local church as well as from members around the world.

We also felt the faith, love, and prayers of many other congregations who reached out on social media. We encourage all to participate in religions that promote love and service to others. We firmly believe in heavenly parents that intimately know us, care for us, and watch over us. We had many, many miracles happen that were far more than coincidences. We received numerous tender mercies from the Lord.

RHETT PRICE. Rhett at the time was an up and coming musician. He reached out to us while Sophie was in rehab at Spaulding Rehabilitation Hospital. Rhett came with his guitarist and played music for an hour for Sophie in Spaulding. They were incredibly talented and it was kind and unselfish for him to do this. He later came to Colchester for a concert we offered to the community as a way to say thank you for all who supported us. Rhett has since enjoyed great success. I encourage you to support his talent.

https://www.facebook.com/rhettypants/
https://www.instagram.com/rhettypants/

YAWKEY FAMILY INN. This was the first place we were able to stay upon arriving at Boston Children's Hospital. We are full of gratitude for having some food and a warm place to stay because of kind strangers donating to provide this Inn to families of sick children.

http://giving.childrenshospital.org/get-involved/volunteer/yawkey-family-inn.html

And now, let me introduce you to Sophie's Song, the inspiring true Christmas story of miracles and music...

Sophie picked up her violin and began to play. It felt good to lay her head on the chinrest.

Up on the House Top then *Rudolph the Red Nosed Reindeer.*

The grandmas and grandpas in the audience smiled to the Christmas music and clapped after each song the violin group played.

Sophie wanted to play her favorite song, *Pachelbel's Canon,* but she had another headache today.

Each slide of Sophie's bow on the violin strings made her headache grow stronger.

She stopped playing and sat down.

Dad walked over and held Sophie close. With her Mom and sister, Lucy, they drove home.

The next day, the headache was worse. Mom drove Sophie to the hospital.

The doctor and nurses took samples of Sophie's blood. They checked her blood pressure and listened to her heart.

They asked her lots of questions, too.

"When did your headache start?"

"Did you bump your head?"

After hours and hours of tests and questions, the doctor walked back in the room.

"A lump in your brain is the cause of your headaches," he said.

Sophie touched the top of her head. It still felt smooth and round.

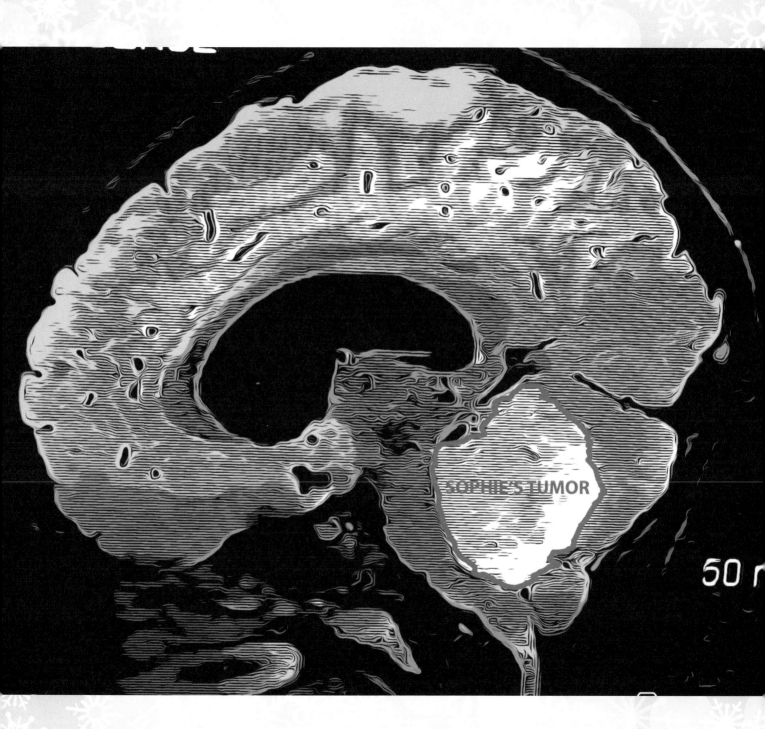

"A team in Boston will be able to operate on you," said the doctor to Sophie and her family.

But Sophie did not understand. Instead, she thought about wrapping presents and driving to White's Christmas Tree Farm to pick out a tree. She thought about Christmas songs, lights, and gifts. She thought about baby Jesus born in a manger.

The doctor left and Sophie's Dad walked out of the room to call family and close friends.

"Will you pray for Sophie," he said to them, trying to be strong through tears.

Mom rode in the ambulance to Boston with Sophie. Dad and Lucy joined them the next day.

New doctors and nurses performed more tests. They said Sophie may not act like her old self after the surgery.

As Sophie waited in her hospital room, Mom made another decision.

"Sophie can finish her concert here."

She called Sophie's violin teacher, and asked her to come to the hospital. Carolyn and all of Sophie's musician friends drove hours through a wintry snow storm to see Sophie.

Wearing hospital pajamas and Santa hat, Sophie entered a room filled with family, TV cameras, Carolyn's violin group, and news reporters from the Boston Globe.

Sophie did not see tears as she played *Away in a Manger* and *We Wish You a Merry Christmas*.

For the finale, Sophie and her friends played Sophie's favorite song, *Pachelbel's Canon*.

Violinists, reporters, friends, and even camera men cried. Sophie concentrated as she played the program to the end.

Sophie's story graced the front page of the Boston Globe. More people learned about her. More people prayed for her and her family.

The next day, Sophie entered the operating room. Dr. Liliana Goumnerova would operate and remove the lump in Sophie's head.

After seven-and-a-half-hours, Dr. Goumnerova spoke to her parents.

"Sophie did well," she said. "But we will need to operate again."

Mom and Dad looked at each other with concern.

"I could not remove the entire lump in one operation," the doctor said.

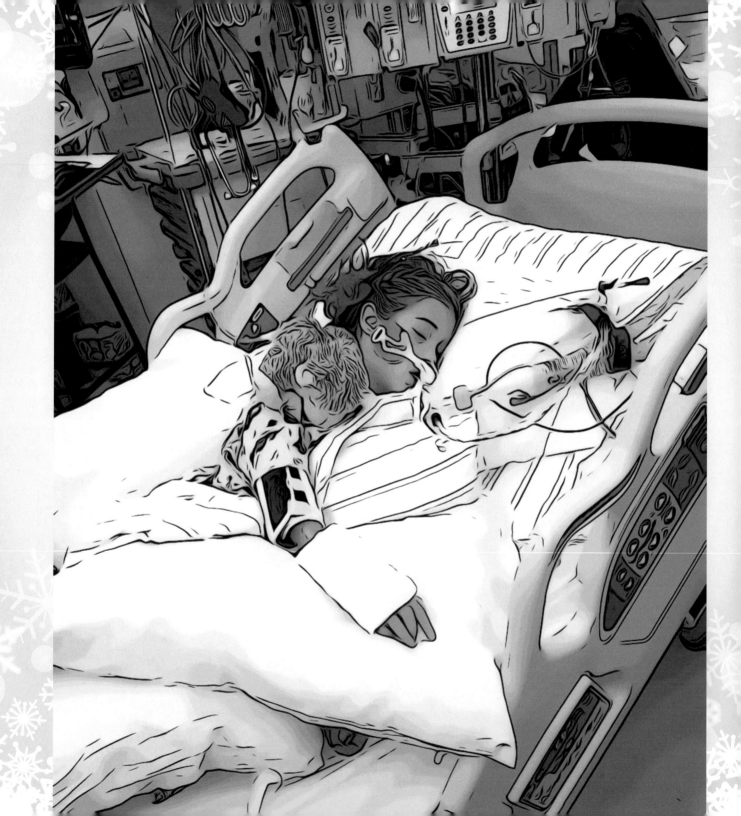

People from all over the country saw the Boston Globe article. An online community followed Sophie's story, too. People who had never met Sophie or her family prayed for her. Those prayers made mom and dad stronger and filled them with hope.

As Dad was walking out of the hospital, *Pachelbel's Canon* played over the hospital speakers. He stopped to listen and felt God's presence. He felt comfort knowing Sophie was being watched over.

Three days later, Dr. Goumnerova told the family her team was ready.

Sophie was barely able to move and afraid to have surgery again.

Another seven and a half hours of waiting.

Success! Dr. Goumnerova was able to remove all of Sophie's tumor. But she was very weak.

Dad looked at Sophie lying in bed. Her body still. Her eyes closed.

"How are you?" Dad asked. She flipped her feeble thumb upward.

Dad left the room. As he walked down the hall, he heard *Pachelbel's Canon* again. He smiled with moistened eyes and paused to thank God.

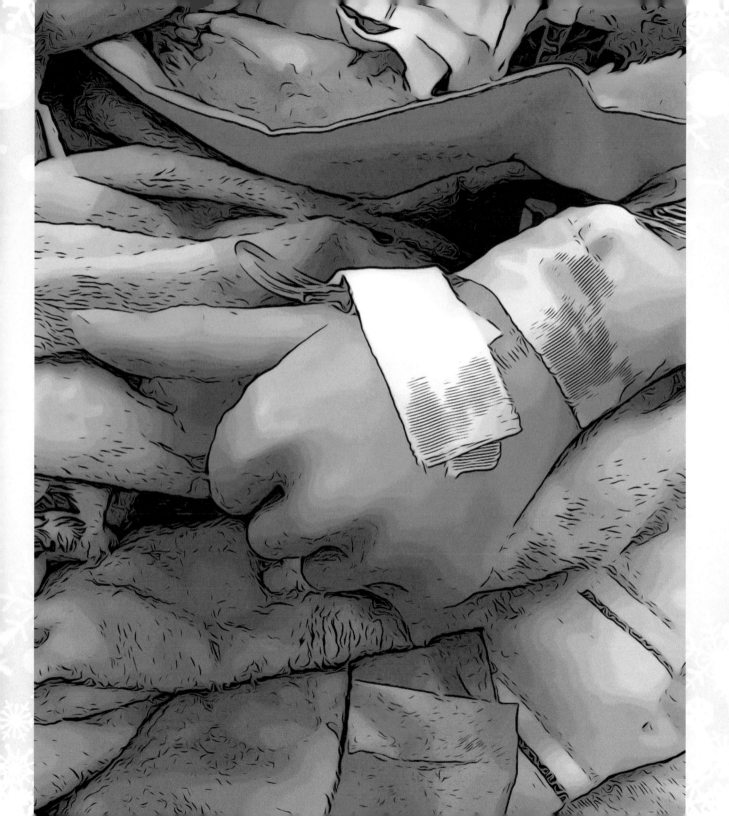

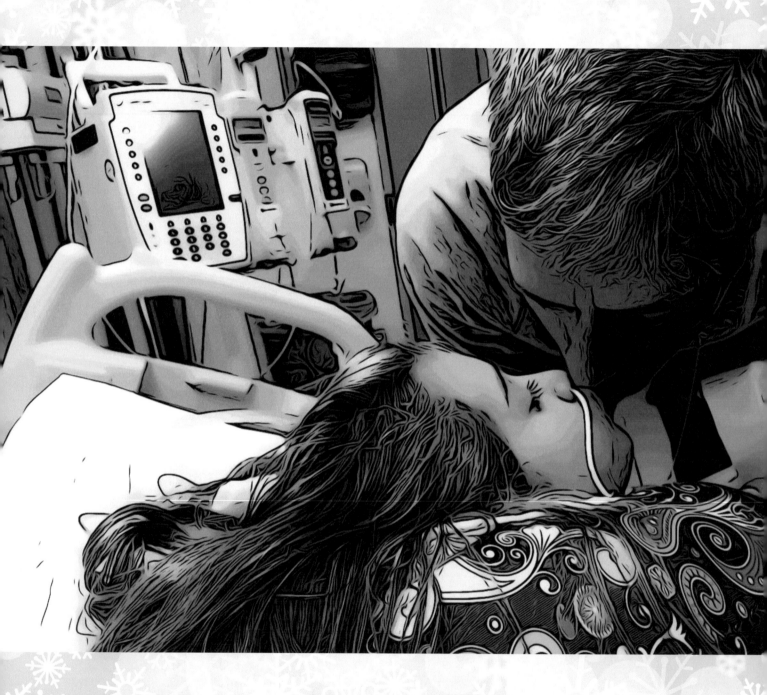

Sophie lay in bed with the airway tube in her throat. She couldn't eat or drink. Her swollen tongue stuck out of her mouth. When she opened her eyes, they crossed.

Her doctors asked her every day: "How many fingers am I holding up?"

"Touch my finger. Now touch your nose. Push against my hands."

The day came for the nurses to remove her airway tube. Sophie could breathe on her own!

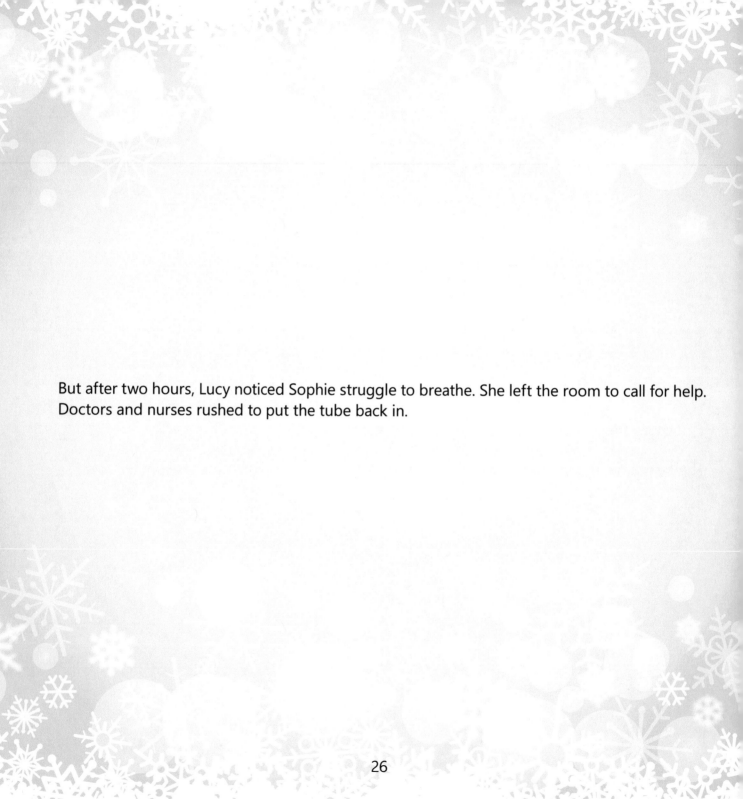

But after two hours, Lucy noticed Sophie struggle to breathe. She left the room to call for help. Doctors and nurses rushed to put the tube back in.

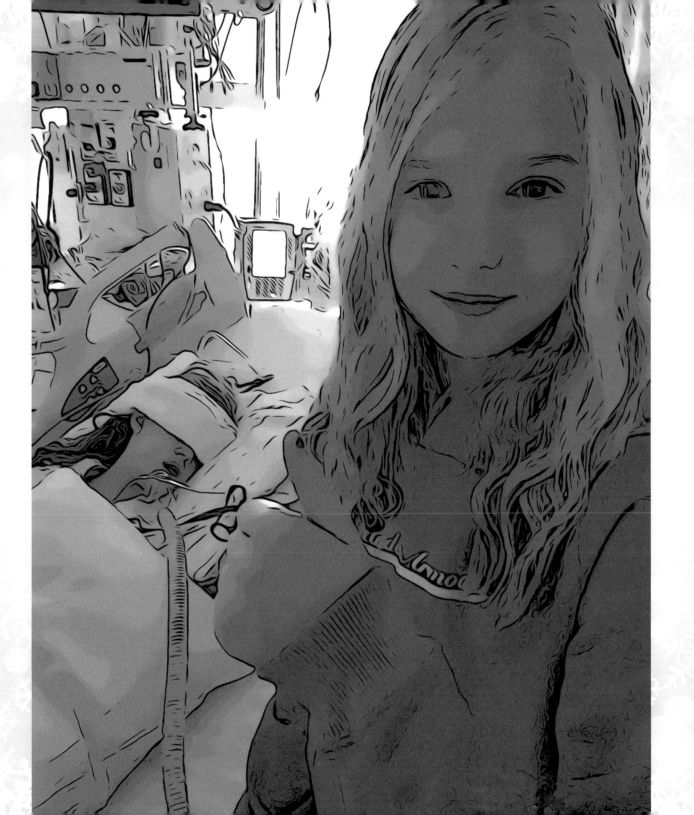

Five days before Christmas, nurses removed the airway tube again. And again, after a few hours, she struggled to breath. The doctors and nurses put the tube back in for a second time.

Sophie's parents could not think about Christmas presents.

They did not sing Christmas carols, or make a Christmas dinner.

They prayed for a Christmas miracle instead.

Dad encouraged everyone who friended Sophie's page on Facebook to pray with him. They did and even offered photos of themselves with their two thumbs up.

Christmas cards taped to the walls brought Sophie and her family loving words.

Caring teachers drove eight hours to visit. Texts, emails, classmates, family, and friends offered hope and prayers.

School groups, firefighters, musicians, military groups, cousins, and dozens more from all over the country sent prayers to Sophie and her family.

Family traveled to Boston from far off places just to hold her hand. Santa even visited Sophie in her hospital room! She was just too weak to celebrate.

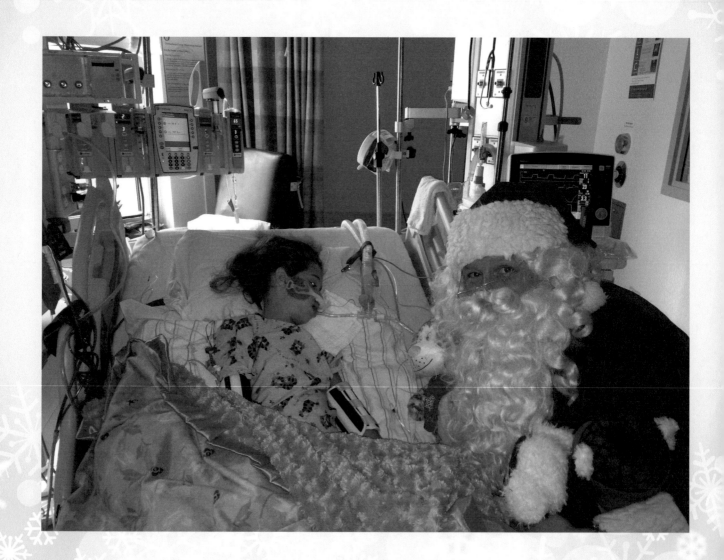

Sophie lay still on Christmas morning. She breathed through the oxygen tube.

Then it happened...

That evening, Sophie became more awakened. She pulled at the tubes that connected her to all the machines. This was EXACTLY what the doctors wanted—a sign she was healing. On this special day we watched Sophie change from lying limp and lifeless to alert and active. A thousand prayers were answered as we witnessed this Christmas miracle!

The next day, Sophie's nurse removed the airway tube. She could breathe on her own.

One year later, Sophie returned to Boston Children's Hospital with her violin friends. They played *Pachelbel's Canon* with Dr. Goumnerova.

The staff and her doctors at Boston Children's hospital healed Sophie. God heard all of the prayers and *Pachelbel's Canon* played.

Addendum

We will continue to give back to local communities and the world as creatively and productively as possible. We hope you all do the same. And if you lack funds, every person on the planet may offer multiple prayers for others. God listens.

Please stay in touch with Sophie by following her Facebook page, Thumbs Up For Sophie. Post a link of you or your group with thumbs up in support of all those who are in a health crisis right now. We hope Sophie's story inspires many people to act, even in small ways, to help someone else in need:

https://www.facebook.com/groups/895096037202470

For author speaking engagements, book signings, Sophie playing violin, donation options to help families in crisis, or to stay in touch with ways we help email: sophiessongbook@gmail.com

Printed in the United States
by Baker & Taylor Publisher Services